THREE FROM
OSAGE STREET

THREE FROM
OSAGE STREET

THOMAS LISENBEE

KAY Z. MYERS

BRET WALLER

authorHOUSE®

AuthorHouse™
1663 Liberty Drive, Suite 200
Bloomington, IN 47403
www.authorhouse.com
Phone: 1-800-839-8640

First published by AuthorHouse   1/8/2009

ISBN: 978-1-4343-8932-9 (sc)

Library of Congress Control Number: 2008905238

Printed in the United States of America
Bloomington, Indiana

This book is printed on acid-free paper.

Photo credits: front cover , p. 11—Ron Breneman; p. 13—Sharon Paige; pp. 16, 18, 38— courtesy of Thomas Lisenbee; p. 45—Brian Canniff; pp. 57, 62, 75, 82 courtesy of Kay Z. Myers; p. 85— Mary Lou Dooley Waller; p. 104—courtesy of Bret Waller; p. 114—courtesy of Jim McCormick

Designed by Bret Waller

Contents

Thomas Lisenbee

Kay Z. Myers

Bret Waller

Biographical Notes

THREE FROM
OSAGE STREET

Catalpas lined our street;
tall, straight ones,
not those crooked dwarfs
you sometimes see,
but towers, thirty, forty meters high,

Bret Waller
North Osage

Planted in anticipation that Girard would spread,
two rows of catalpas towered yet
above flat Kansas fields of frost-brown weeds.

Kay Z. Myers
Trees

Home, after all,
is only another way of saying Osage Street.

Thomas Lisenbee
Osage Street

Thomas Lisenbee

*for Evelyn and Percy, for Ranulf and Calin,
for Ulrika, Pete and Melanie, for Phoebe and Phil and Emil
and most especially, for my meadowlark wife, Sharon*

Osage Street

Osage Street. A warm summer evening caught in the crack between day and night. A small-for-his-age, barefoot boy, sitting on the steps of his front porch watching and listening as his street gets ready to go to sleep. One of my poems in this book begins this way. That boy of course is me and the street is Osage Street. In other poems, the cicadas are humming, the starlings are raising hell in the Courthouse square, in a few minutes my father may suggest going to O'Reilly's for ice cream. Osage Street begets heavy memories: the strange inedible fruit of the buckeye tree in the Kellys' front yard next door, sweet blossoms sucked freshly plucked from our catalpa tree; memories of fat-tired, over-used cars made of real steel with white-walls and heavily chromed bumpers, bearing names like Packard and Cadillac parked in our driveway by my father; memories of the Kelly boys' junk yard; alpine memories of scrambling ascents and tumbling descents of corn cob piles. Memories that, made into poems, fit into the palm of your hand; or perhaps a brew to sip for the rest of your life. There is no part of this distillate world that is not right.

Although the houses on my block were plain, simple, modest, you might say working man's utilitarian, their inhabitants were anything but. We all seemed to be uniquely interesting in some way. Kay's grandmother she writes so lovingly about, lived around the corner from us, on Walnut Street no more than forty yards away. Grandma and Grandpa Zettls' bakery not only fed and perfumed our town but entertained this young boy as well because ensconced in the bakery's front window was the marvelous doughnut machine. Paul Sell lived in a big house across the alley from Kay's grandmother. He ran one of the town's two appliance stores and much to the sorrowing of my father's stomach, played electric organ and the soprano sax. Then there was erstwhile businessman Walter Wayland. His 5 & 10 included a used comic book market but his real passion was composing march music. He was our local John Philip Sousa. His magnum opus? A march called, for no known reason, "Billy Possum."

My block on Osage Street was close to the Courthouse square, the town's omphalos, the town's fulcrum upon which all life balanced for miles around.

Walk one block down Walnut to Summit, turn right at the First Christian Church where my mother was the director of the choir, walk one more block and there was the square.

How I loved Saturdays. Every parking place taken. The sidewalks filled with people who knew each other. Farmers from miles around, come into town to drop their shopping lists off at their favorite grocery stores while they shopped for clothes at Sauer's, or perhaps took in a matinee movie at the Cozy Theater—a few of whom were sure to be at the Cozy on Wednesday night when we all had the same chance to win twenty four silver dollars.

This is the house at 203 Osage I lived in from age five. Next door is the house we were renting when I was born, owned by Mr. and Mrs. Woods during the time they were still operating Woods' Hotel and presumably living there. During most of the war years we lived on South Summit in the big old tumbledown house owned by the Fox Sisters, aunts to the unforgettable John Henry. A house some readers of this book may remember because after we moved out, among the many furnishings the Fox sisters brought with them when they moved in, was the life-sized papier mâché horse that, in my mind, forever stands in glory on that front porch.

Then there was the other Osage Street that began farther up, past the High School, up where Kay and Bret lived. The fancy part of town, as my parents used to say, where rich people lived—meaning of course, the Sauers. Up where some people kept horses in their yards. Up where the houses were larger and grander and kids had only to walk mere minutes to Burnett's or McFarland's Lake to go fishing or for fooling around. Exciting things seemed to happen there. Like following the fire truck to watch Bret's barn burn down. It's where the catalpas pictured on the cover of this book, escort Osage Street up to where it curves around into Summit. And in the bend of that curve there used to be a small pond between the road and the railroad tracks, where small boys threw rocks at snapping turtles and snakes and frogs, where I later took Mabel Roper, whom I was sweet on at the time, ice skating. Those double rows of catalpas were planted because someone had a vision once of Girard growing and growing, but alas, the only things that kept growing and growing were those catalpa trees. We lost the elms. The sidewalk, intended to run between those twin rows didn't so much end abruptly, as peter out.

I remember this summer's day. Sitting on my front porch steps with three of my friends. All of us still in grade school, maybe the fourth or fifth grade, and we began talking about serious things. Like where we wanted to live when we grew up, and I remember saying: Girard was the perfect size. McCune and Cherokee were too small. Pittsburg was too big, but Girard had everything. I ticked off a long list—the Cozy Theater, a swimming pool, a first class Post Office, two train stations, we were the County Seat, we were class A in sports. Now, I have no idea why I said what I said next, but in all seriousness, I said this: the one place I would never ever live was New York City. And then, I remember, we scrunched our faces the way we did at the movies whenever Van Johnson kissed June Allyson.

Well, I guess I might as well say it. I tempted fate; I paid the price. I came to Brooklyn in 1966 and never left. In full disclosure, I should admit I feel as much at home in Brooklyn as I once did in Kansas. True I have a country home now on the Delaware River where I can go to listen to the cicadas. We even have a catalpa tree planted there. Beside the road, of course. Yes, I love the city. But contrary to belief, New York City is not a sprawling, overwhelming, heartless metropolis so much as a complex concatenation of crazy quilt neighborhoods—imagine the towns of Crawford County, their integrity preserved, minus the farmland. My neighborhood in Brooklyn is called Red Hook. I moved there in 1984. And the day I turned onto Van Brunt Street to go take a first look at the house I would later buy, I was struck by how like Girard this neighborhood was. My god, no traffic lights and there were utility poles strung with all sorts of wires. Wouldn't you know it, my house had to be on Pioneer Street where, yes, people all seem to know each other, or know to act like it anyway. While there is no Billy Possum in Red Hook, I found a dead raccoon on the street one time. But it was the day I laughed to hear a mockingbird try his best to pass for a meadowlark, when it all seemed to make sense. Home, after all, is only another way of saying Osage Street.

Tootin' Tommy

Sonnet

The distant sounds of children playing, a passing
train, a barking dog; inside our home
the muffled clatter of supper dishes being
washed; an absent neighbor's unanswered phone,
a car whines up a hill and flashing fireflies
blend their counterpoint rhythm to the tree
frogs choral fugue. And gently summoned by
the tranquil magic of this night, the memories
of my sweet youth forsake their dusty shelf
to form themselves into the ranks and files
of a small-town parade. Beside myself,
like some excited child, with glee I smile
and follow them until once more I dance
through time into my boyhood town in Kansas.

The Things I Remember

I remember an honest-to-god small
town that could have been a back lot
stunt double for Pleasantville or Grover's Corners.

I remember an authentic town square
around a county courthouse where my
father's town band played concerts in the summer.

I remember you could walk everywhere.
I remember brick streets named after Indian tribes.
I remember massive elm trees and stately catalpas.

I remember the old brick building
on the southwest corner of the square
carried the faded logo of Fogel's Harness Factory.

I remember a whole bunch of churches.
I remember a rowdy summer church softball
league where we ignored our theological differences.

I remember the Catholic priest drove a Studebaker
Hawk with straight-pipe cut-out; I remember good kids
hung out in the drug store, bad kids in the pool hall.

I remember the night we stuffed pigeons through
the high school mail chute. I remember the morning
after the night someone piled our books on the study hall stage.

I remember the night Marlin Viets got hit on the
top of the head with a gob of chewing tobacco under
the bleachers during a Friday night football game.

I remember some farms didn't have electricity, some
sections of town, indoor-plumbing; how boys took shop
or industrial arts, how girls took home economics and typing.

I remember the Cozy Theater, Nick's Drive Inn
and Decker's Diner. I remember the little forest,
Burnett's pond, my tree house, my butterfly collection.

I remember old streetcar tracks, horse tanks
and a barber/mayor called Bat Ginzell. I remember
O'Reilly's Drug Store held turtle races every summer.

I remember other people used firecrackers
and pots and pans to scare the starlings away;
my folks used the cymbals from my father's marching band.

I remember Evan's Motors sold Mrs. Murray a barber-pole
red and white '56 Plymouth and how we laughed when she asked us
where she lived, because none of us understood Alzheimer's.

I remember the slide and swings at Winston Park,
Bat Ginzell's Amateur Hour, swimming lessons.
I remember things never celebrated.

I remember how 'colored' children never swam
in our town pool. How William Jennings Bryan
was said to have fallen asleep on the Turners' front porch.

How the *Appeal to Reason* was published in Girard.
How E. Haldeman-Julius invented the paper
back book of which he sold over fifty million.

I remember my grandmother once lived
in a sod house. I remember my mother and father
remembered the Dust Bowl and the Great Depression.

I remember the joy I felt leaving in 1960,
I remember the sadness in coming back to find
something missing or someone forgotten.

But most of all I remember weeping the day
I returned to put a red rose on each of my parent's graves;
because someone unknown had left flowers before me;

because it drove this truth home:
when you come from a small town,
you come from an island of remembering.

My Father's Rocker

It was his throne. The place he sat when
he gave music lessons or repaired
instruments or listened to a St. Louis Cardinals
baseball game. I don't know where or how he came by it.
Perhaps on one of those mysterious
trips of his to see a man about a dog
that for some reason he never brought home.

I have the rocker still. But I don't sit in it often.
Because it belongs to him.   But when I do and
close my eyes, I am that boy whose feet hardly
touched the floor and sat in it to listen
to Sky King and the Lone Ranger.

The wood still carries a hint of the scent
it absorbed from him—the staleness of sour-mash
and cigarettes and growing old—and I remember
the day I displeased him when I used my decoder ring
and the back page of his baseball ledger to transcribe
a secret message from Sky King and Penny and Clipper,
eating raw potatoes salt and peppered by
my mother, knowing I'll have to give the rocker
up to him as soon as he comes home.

IT

*....my dearest faith has been that this
is but a trial. I shall be changed.*
                    Stanley Kunitz

It was during those mystery disaster years,
when every misery seemed fated, that three
sapling boys, smack dab between childhood
and coming on to be men, decided to ride
their bikes to Farlington Lake one summer day:
Richard Baldwin, someone forgotten and myself.

I don't know who first thought of swimming
the quarter mile from the tower to the dock
then back again. It couldn't have been me
because they were strong swimmers and I
was not; because, of all the boys who took
swimming lessons together, I was the one whose
muscles failed to strengthen and harden; because,
during subsequent games of tag at the town pool,
it was the runt, not the water rat, best suited to be *It.*

Richard was the first to balance the pipe
to the tower, then the other kid, then myself.
They dove straight away and struck for the dock.
I followed strong—their enthusiasm pulled me along,
perhaps this was my day—then my arms began
getting tired and I realized there was no lifeguard
keeping watch, no nearby fisherman in a boat;
I was out there and this was some serious business.
So I abandoned the Australian Crawl for less exhausting
strokes; at times I floated, and when I dared to check,
there was no longer any advantage to turning back.

They were waiting for me to touch the dock,
welcomed my arrival like seals on a rock;
barking, clapping, ready to dive, ready to arc,
because it was that accursed game again and,
exhausted or not, fool or not, I had no choice. Our
bikes were near the tower so I flopped into their wake.

I would like to say they cheered my return to the tower,
          but they did not.
I would like to say that day I proved myself their equal,
          but I had not.
I would like to say that day a grubby worm became a butterfly,
          but it did not.

There were to be more years of feeling lower caste, of thinking
a ship had sailed and I'd been left behind, of playing right field,
an *It* too small too shy to dare a kiss or ask for a date.

But we did grow up. All of us. Some bloom late.

Our senior year I was co-captain of the track
team and Richard Baldwin and I were one half
of a 4x440 relay team that set the league record.
Richard died last year. He was a clever boy.
He became a doctor. And how can I speak of my
other friend when I can't remember his face or
his name; only the nut-brown sparkling sun-dripping
sheen of him and the turban he made of his t-shirt;
because I struggle over that swim at Farlington Lake
the way a befuddled convict puzzles an unjust trial.
I risked my life not because I was brave and strong
but because I feared the shame of not-swimming
more. Because we *are* all alike. It's the oldest
game, as simple as crossing against the light.

Playing tag with death.   Celebrating life.

Horseshoes

The boy is barefoot, alone, or maybe, better said, fresh run out of friends.
The smith is a giant of a giant of a giant of a man. Broad-chested, leather-
aproned, brawny-armed, the smith is, as his father has been and his
grandfather before that, blacksmith to the town clear back to the finial days
of Fogel's harness factory.

Smoke from the chimney informs the boy the smithy works the forge. It
is the brobdingnagian cowskin bellows that draws the boy to stand in the
door. Air witched *sturm* and *drang* through a nozzle sets iron roasting from
red to yellow-almost-white before the smith submits it to anvil and the
debauching of molecules begins. Banging, clanging, whanging the iron,
then the snarling, snavial hiss of it plunged into a ready vat of dirty water; a
beatification, a rebaptism completed from what once was into something or
something or something or other.

Iron, the boy's dictionary says, *the commonest and most useful metal, from
which tools and machinery, etc are made.* But the boy working the bellows
is wise to more than that. A forge is an underworld where this god and a
dwarf like him mutilate immutable magic. The story of shaping iron is the
story of creation. He knows this must be so. His encyclopedia tells him:
Lord Vulcan is the husband of Venus.

I sit alone...

in the heat of a soft summer's night,
rummaging the back closet of my mind,
until I find myself a barefoot boy again,
sitting on the steps of my front porch in Kansas.

My mother is in the kitchen,
my father listening to a St. Louis Cardinals game.
Today I went to the little forest
on the west edge of town just off Walnut Street.

The crawdads I caught there
are out back of our garage,
hidden from my mother
in the withering misery of an old coffee can.

The little forest is a wild place
where wild boys do wild things;
a half-block overgrown
with small catalpas, bushes and tall grasses;

our Burnham Wood, our Sherwood Forest,
a place to go by day but never at night;
a place where caves have secret entrances,
where booby-traps protect us from invaders.

And beside a little stream,
there is one tree worthy of the name,
that is massive and straight and true—
an aged cottonwood that is our jungle gym,
our mizzenmast, our beanstalk to a giant's lair—
underneath which, today, we did a strange new thing.

We built a fire and removed all our clothes
and danced like savages in a way we never would again.
The world, we will too soon find out,
is somewhat more than a little forest.

A place where themes
have too many variations
and freedom,
like war, is a gnarly word.

The Flood

The road disappeared into the still brown water that cloudless
    sunny day we left the car at the barrier and started walking.

It was August. The heat was brutal.   He said *where are your shoes*
    but I said *no, my feet are callused.* I ended up hopping.

At water's edge, I turned my head and he motioned me into the tepid
    silted water. I watched my toes disappear, then my feet, then my ankles.

That's far enough, son, he cautioned through his cigarette, his fedora
    tipped back, his lanky frame turned by the sun into smoky silhouette.

I knew where the river was. You could tell by a row of trees and the top
    of the bridge. I had imagined worse. I had seen Hollywood's version

of Noah's Flood and pictures in *Life* and *Look* of frightful, roiling rivers,
    but this one, the Neosho, my first to see in flood, had spread

easy upon the land like a drunken, courtly gentleman. Small fish hurried
    across the road. I heard raucous laughter.

Hidden by a hedgerow, a murder of crows mocked the murky
    outline of a sunken tractor. I felt safe but disappointed.

There was no hint of final days. No fear of being swept away.
    But this was in my beginning time when there were no angry rivers.

Campin' Out

We pitch our tent by a stream; he's only six or eight;
the hour is late afternoon and the air warm and still.

I follow the sun to a large stone slab; he chases
minnows in the shallows. We talk of things
he finds and places we have been; *why this,*
he wants to know, *how come* or *what is that.*

I close my eyes and weave a mantra from the music
of a brook, the hum of a bee, the sweet obligato of a bird.

My son skips stones across the water. There's a blindman's
wait for them to arc from hand to pool. I savor the stutter
of the stone, the varied shades of kerplunk. A tiny breeze
flutters past my cheek...is this dream complete?

Time rides a slow horse across this gentle earth.

Sensing we are not alone, I open my eyes and see my son
sitting beside the ferns; his hand before him, he offers
a crust of bread to the inquisitive nose of a curious rabbit.

I marvel that my hobbit son, his cap pulled so low
he has butterfly's wings for ears, can wizard such a spell.
He turns to me and smiles. He is not amazed.

In his cartoon world, Bambi and Thumper behave this way.
My father took me camping only once; and it was too hot

and the tent was smelly and small
and when I went to a place
he told me not to go, I was chased
through her wallow by an angry old sow.

My son is a father now.
I've held his child in my arms.
I would give anything
to ride with them
in the rumble seat
of my father's old car,
just the four of us,
going for ice cream,
then driving to the woods

and campin' out.

Reunion

A message
A simple request
A name: Carol
A class reunion

Fifty years

and we are barefoot once more
    running through the grass on Osage Street

catching fireflies

putting them in a bottle

set on her back step

a magic lantern

our lives-to-be

restless points of light

My Fiftieth High School Reunion—The Uncertainty Principle

When I entered the room, my graduating class had dwindled to about the size of an infantry platoon. We had lost eleven. Some twenty odd were missing in action.

> Cleaning out my shed is a twice a year project,
> elsewise there would never
> be room to turn around.
> It's during these cleaning out times I screwdriver
> open my old paint cans
> to see how much paint is left inside.

In a keepsake photo taken in the gym, they make us sit on the bleacher steps like children. Where are the teachers, I think, when I receive my copy in the mail.

> Opening the can may be more archeology
> than assessment. We know in advance the paint
> will be covered with a thick rubbery film.
> Too much air keeps it that way.

You don't have enough signatures, my wife says
when she checks my souvenir book.
You must get more, she urges,
or they will think you think them not important.

> The trick is to break the film with a stick
> and fish out as much of the muck as you can,
> then give the rest a good stir to coax
> the color into changing tenses.
> At this point comes the decision—
> throw it away or save it for another day.

Heady stuff isn't it, I think, surveying a face not seen for fifty years,
being assayed by length of tooth, the pallor and texture of our skin,
the quality and quantity of the hair remaining on our heads?

Puzzling isn't it, this not letting go, I blurt to the girl who sat behind me in
study hall my senior year. *You haven't changed at all,* she says referring, I
suppose, to how I used to annoy her by putting my elbow on her desk.

Satisfied,
I tap the lid tight;
I'll return this can to my shed.

This is the kitchen.....

Nothing of value here
No antiques
The fridge is not new

> *They called it an icebox.*

The stove is hardly better

> *She kept a can of bacon grease on that stove*

These pots and pans won't bring much
These cabinets look home-made
Old Percy was not much of a carpenter was he?

> *But he was a master of making do*
> *They are gone*
> *The people who used to eat in this room are gone*
> *Evelyn and Percy and what was their child's name?*

What's in there?
Where?
Behind that door
A pantry and a toilet

> *That's where Percy kept his whiskey and Evelyn smoked her Kools*
> *She'd fan the air   turn her back   flush the butt*
> *to hide it from her son*
> *She wanted to be a singer or an actress but she had duties*
> *and was never free*
> *"For medicinal purposes only," he'd say to the boy, then wink*
> *and replace the cap*
> *He'd had his shot playing fiddle in the roaring twenties in KC*

No pictures, linoleum, plain light fixtures, three blue chairs
Withered ivy plant on the gnarled table, old green ashtray beside the sink.

This is where she stood to wash the dishes
See the floor register above?
The boy used to lie there and ask her over and over
as if the needle were stuck on the gramophone they didn't have
Do you love me, do you love me, do you love me, do you love me, mama, do you
love me
And she always gave him the same indifferent reply

Looks like that boy took the good stuff back east with him
and left the rest............for us to auction.

ODE on a photograph found among my mother's effects

Picture three young women.
Picture them properly dressed
in nineteen-twenties
modest flapper finery.
Picture light cloth coats.
Picture the pelt of one
small animal as a furry boa.
Picture tidy felt hats.
One sports a feather.
Picture saggy black hosiery,
chunky high heels.
Picture them ready
for a date or church.
Add a vintage oil truck,
a Model A perhaps.
In the cab of this truck
sits a man, his face
lost in deep shadow.
But it is not this man
we are interested in
but one of our three
arrayed muses, perched
sidesaddle atop the tank,
their badinage temporarily
arrested by the camera.

One perhaps just after saying,
 whose idea is this anyway?
Or maybe to the photographer,
 take this picture quick.
Delight shows.
 Isn't this jolly, great fun?
Picture sepia.

The one in the middle is plainly a woman on stage,
a coquette looking over her shoulder playing to the camera.
I am drawn to her because I sense she must be my mother,
yet even with the aid of a magnifying glass I cannot be sure.
But I want her to be my mother, the before mother,
the-person-I-never-knew mother, the unrealized version
my mother sacrificed to get on to life and raising a child.

To know my mother in this blossoming moment.
To celebrate life before the heavy stuff begins. What dreams
she must have—the stage, New York City, singing, acting?—
because she has the talent, the desire, what she doesn't
get are the breaks. The Depression, the Second
World War, a brother to help through college to an
Ivy League graduate degree, a husband deathly sick
she'll nurse for years, a child to raise; for such
would be her knuckled life on Osage Street.

Yet, she was well prepared for cheery sacrifice, for
sublimating all her talents into a teaching career.
My mother grew up on a wheat farm of good
German/Welsh stock. My mother knew work.
She knew endurance. She knew tornadoes, dust storms,
plagues of grasshoppers; she knew raising tomatoes.

She knew rising at four in the morning at threshing time
to help her mother and grandmother prepare food enough
to feed three meals to a small army of field hands.
My mother grew up without electricity, indoor plumbing,
or cooking gas; no trees, no fancy lawn, no telephone,
the nearest tiny town miles away.

So look closer, the truck's rear wheels wear chains
even though it is plainly spring, possibly summer;
but remember in dust-stricken western Kansas,
where my mother grew up and this photo was
probably taken, flash rains turn dirt roads to rutted muck
making them well nigh impassable. Spoke-wheeled,
jaunty box cab, this truck, as much as she, a marvel
of perseverance and determination. Picture my mother
jumping from haylofts onto stacks of freshly mown hay.

Author's note: I have had great difficulty in writing directly about my mother. I think, because there
was very little friction between us, I always took her for granted. The irony is, the inspiration for this
piece, this photo that became the portal for getting to the very thing I wanted to say about her, upon
closer examination with a proper photographer's magnifying lens proved conclusively that none of
these women is my mother and the shadowy man in the cab, is, of course, the shadow that has driven
and supported me my whole life, my father. What to say, but in art, such things happen.

My first bicycle had a broken head set.
I could lift the handlebars clear out as I pedaled
and hold them like antlers above my head.

1)

I'm lying on my back on the carpet. My eyes are closed.
I'm doing what I do best: listening to the sounds of my family
as they move about their one room cabin at the edge of the woods.

Phil is scratching like a cat in his Lego box.
He's Spiderman these days and is probably building
a spideyopolis he'll web up later with cars.

Pete is at the computer, designing showrooms for Mt. Blanc
or Cartier or Lanvin. If it weren't for the rain he'd be outside,
an internal combustion engine throbbing in his hands.

And in the corner, where the light is best,
where the long table sits, I hear the whoops and sobs
of the Ladies Triparte Generational Jigsaw Puzzle Fest.

Mother, Daughter, Grandmother. An impossibly devilish puzzle
of a Puppy in a Tea Cup. They must be stuck;
they've been at it so long, they've given some of the pieces names.

I never was a puzzler, perhaps such visioning is a womanly
thing: a sport for witches and sorceresses. I was builder of model planes
and trains, and ships and cars. A collector too. Matchbooks, butterflies,
Indian-head pennies, stamps, bars of hotel soap, marbles, pop bottle caps.
Pep pins (I sent away for the beanie hat), baseball cards (I hated the gum:)
the otiose pelf of a barefoot youth spent wearing holes in my jeans.

My mother never did a puzzle; I never saw my father lying on the floor.
There were only the three of us, and never a cabin in the woods.
Things happened to us in a car. The day the bee flew in the window
for instance and my father's cigarette fell into the crotch of his pants:
the car veering to the side of the road, his open door, my mother and I
laughing at my father's strange hopping dance, the wind in his hair.

I once made a large corrugated box into a theater
And performed for them magic and puppet shows.

2)

This was supposed to be the year
 of the seventeen-year cicada.
Seventeen. Not a Fibonacci number
but a prime just the same.
Evidently evolution chose this odd time-cycle
for them so those looking to eat cicadas
might choose something else for dinner—
unpredictability, a defense.

In Kansas, our cicadas came every year.
A different breed, probably.
The trunk of our Catalpa thick with them—
delicately green and shiny wet
before they flew away from their split-out shells.
And sing. They did sing:
so loudly they competed with the starlings
that flocked each night to the courthouse square.
Summer evenings were noisy in Girard, Kansas.
But this year in Pennsylvania,
the cicadas brought us silence.
I was hungry to hear them.

It slips by so easily:
the collecting of cicada shells from the bark of a catalpa,
my first bicycle, the magic shows
I performed for my father and mother.
Laughter and words fitted into the completion of a puzzle,
my step-daughter's family, this good cabin.

Some day I will enter these woods,
leave my split-out shell, complete my cycle.
My son and daughter live far away.
Ranulf. Calin.
We give our children names
so in our sea of solitude
they swim back to us,
so families flow like water.

Kindness

Sunset anywhere is that long goodbye that is never long enough. First, the windowless room and the silent nun who kept him company while the hospital staff made his mother presentable for viewing. Then his mother, hardly noble, her body only a remnant she had left behind, so strangely pale and bloated, her forehead cold as marble when eventually he kissed it and said goodbye. Then he called Ruth, his mother's best friend, and told her he was starting the three hour drive from Wichita to the house he no longer called home. It was winter dark when he got into his car, past midnight when he arrived, and he was amazed to see nearly every window filled with light and Ruth waiting in the living room together with his mother's closest friends. She had turned up the heat. They were there, she said, so he wouldn't have to enter a cold and darkened house.

Small Things

The rustle of dry leaves,
A blade of grass in a summer breeze,
A frog in a pond, distant birdsong
Are only small things.

A neighbor's call from a passing car
Black nights filled with so many stars,
Wildflowers huddled in a ditch,
These are small things.

An evening spent cutting grass,
A meadowlark, a chrysalis,
A helping hand, the high school band,
Such very small things.

An eddy in a river or brook
A fleeting glance, a second look
Three feet of snow, no place to go
The exquisite insignificance of small things.

A life well lived, a cemetery
filled with relatives and friends,
A tree no one wants to cut down,
As it is with these, so it is with our small town.

Kay Z. Myers

with love to John and all my other family, past, present, and future

Childhood Memories

I. *First Day of School*

I was to enter first grade early. Instead, I nearly died
(ruptured appendix) and lost a year to naps
and nasty-tasting tonics and loneliness for
my friend, Joan, who started school without me.
So I had little sympathy for Jerry's tears
on my first day of school. Gary, the tall, fat boy
who walked to school with me, chased him
for several afternoons, taunting, "Crybaby, cry!"
I watched and never said a word—but felt
somehow responsible, ashamed.

II. *The Walk to School*

Much of the next twelve years, I walked that selfsame block
to school and back twice daily. Returning, I passed
the tidy house with crowing roosters and a picket fence
that made a lovely click-clack song when someone
ran a stick along it. The next house belonged to Mary Jane,
who, at my age plus three, was generally too old
to be of interest—though I *was* interested when
she showed me her blisters. (Recently, a nurse had
given scratch tests to the entire elementary school—
a big event!) Mary Jane said blisters didn't mean
she had TB, just that she'd been exposed.
The Bailey's house came next. On May Days,
I dropped a construction-paper basket full of flowers
at their front door, then rang the bell and hid.
The fun was in their mock surprise. The last house
on that block (catty-cornered from my own)
was a ramshackle, empty place, its yard waist-high
in weeds. "A hide-out for hobos," Gary said.

III. *Wichita*

When Grandma Tindal had an operation, Mother
took me and went to Wichita to care for her.
I still recall that diabolical merry-go-round at one
of the school playgrounds: push, hop, and ride;
push, hop, and ride—until, dizzy and nauseated,
I came back home to Grandma's and queasy dreams
of whirligigs. When I woke up with measles,
Grandma and I recuperated jointly.
She read me *The Adventures of Tom Sawyer*—
and I was gloriously afraid of Injun Joe.

IV. *My Cousin Judy*

The spring Daddy was drafted and stationed
at Camp Lee, Virginia, Mother went to visit him
and left me in Lawrence, Kansas, with Aunt Frances
and Uncle Doc. My cousin Judy had an electric train
and a doll house with electric lights—wonders
which seemed *almost* a compensation
for lost parents.

Judy could eat egg yolks and I could tolerate the whites—
so, breakfasting alone, we usually managed
to clean up our plates. I do recall, however, struggling
through one breakfast of poached eggs
while Auntie's cleaning woman regaled us with tales
of the medicinal virtues of eating chicken shit.

After school one day, Judy and I went off to play
across the street, but we forgot to tell Aunt Frances.
When asked if I should share her spanking,
Judy said no, she was to blame—but, privately,
she told me that I *should* have been spanked too.
When we girls got chicken pox together, the doctor

48

came. Learning from Auntie that I wished to be a boy,
he said, "I've heard if girls can kiss their elbows . . ."
I found that, double-jointed, I *could* kiss my elbow—
but I remained a girl.

V. *Petersburg*

In Petersburg, Virginia, that summer, Mother
checked out a wartime rental while I swung
from a tree limb with the resident child.
During my turn, the large limb broke, and the boy
drawled, "Man, will my dad ever be mad at you!"
Before I left, we dragged the limb into a ditch behind his house.

To my relief, we didn't rent there after all, but moved
into a second-floor apartment with the wife and daughters
of Daddy's army friend. There, we three girls waved
to the engineer each time the train passed through
the street below; we hassled the black maid;
we visited a neighbor, an artist who had,
in her apartment, a life-sized, self-portrait—nude.
In the Virginia heat, she let us strip down
to our underpants, mark our flat chests with lipstick,
and play at Tarzan and the natives.
She taught us the card game, Authors, which,
in that exotic setting, sparked my lifelong
romance with classic literature.

Daddy carved for me a wooden gun and dagger,
so we girls played army in the hedged-in yard.
Later, our parents drove us to spend a weekend
at Virginia Beach. Bored and half carsick,
I played the alphabet game, stamped white horses,
counted telephone poles . . . then, *voilà*!
The vast, magnificent ocean!
Bluer than Kansas skies—

so bright I couldn't look square on—
rowdy with surf and gulls—
smelling uniquely ripe with promise!
A small landlubber, I was irrevocably
smitten with the sea.

September came; I started second grade in Petersburg.
There, I was rescued from a crayon-snatcher
by a barefoot gentleman in knickers
(unheard of apparel in Girard)
who stealthily crawled down the aisle
and stole my crayons back. There, to my great
mortification, I was kept after school to master
cursive writing. When we returned to Kansas,
a worse embarrassment awaited—
I had to print again.

VI. *Confession*

For months, I'd suffered from the guilt
of hiding that blasted broken limb.
Now, home again, I finally confessed—
and found such easy absolution that,
for years thereafter, Mother
became my comfortable confessor.

VII. *Meditations on Infinity*

I was a budding theologian and wondered,
on my walks to school, who started God?
What came before Creation if one went back
and back and back? While I ate breakfast oatmeal
once, an answer popped into my head: since
I accepted Heaven that kept going on and on,
day after day, why not accept a God who
kept on going in the opposite direction?

This satisfied my childish thoughts sufficiently
that I moved on to ponder other problems—
though, for some years, I tended
to associate infinity with oatmeal.

VIII. *The Track Meet*

Our yearly track meet with Emerson
set all of Lowell Elementary racing, jumping,
and throwing balls. Lowell usually lost, but never mind!
Each spring brought hope, proffered potential heroes.
Spending the night together, Joan and I sang
silly love songs to Lowell's best high-jumper:
"Oh my darling, oh my darling,
oh my darling Johnnie T . . ."

IX. *Chickens*

When Mother and Daddy left for a weekend
bakery convention in Kansas City, I had to walk
from Joan's to feed our hens and gather eggs.
The nesting chickens stared at me . . .
and stared . . .
and stared . . .
and stared . . .
Hens have such awful eyes—
reptilian, impersonal, malicious.
Each time I gathered courage . . .
to reach into a nest . . .
the hen pecked me!
I donned my father's leather gloves,
gingerly retrieved the eggs—
and salvaged my self-respect.

X. *Fishing the Creek*

Daddy rigged me a seat
in an old inner tube and towed me
down the creeks he waded fly-fishing.
I liked being outdoors, being with him.
The water filled my tennis shoes and squished
about my toes when I climbed out.
Fishing Sunday mornings, though, I felt
that I should be in church instead.

XI. *Mary Lou*

For several special summers, Mary Lou Wasser came
from Chicago to stay with her two maiden aunts;
and I drew whole families of paper dolls for Mary Lou,
Joan, Alice Ann, and me. Sitting atop rush rugs
in Wassers' basement, we outlined clothes-pin houses
for our play. We knew that we were lucky—
that this clean, concrete basement was much cooler
than any other place in town except the swimming pool
or, possibly, the library. Though we played much indoors,
Aunt Ida and Aunt Louisa's yard was one of the best
groomed in Girard. Reputedly, they grew
such lovely flowers because
on dark nights, demurely, they collected fertilizer
from Brenemans' pony lot next door.

XII. *The Boys Next Door*

Ronnie Breneman and Bret Waller (my age
plus two and three) were not at all too old
to be of interest. Ronnie had a bag swing,
a weeping willow tree, a basketball hoop, a pony.
I found both him and his possessions altogether
admirable. He shot my hair, once, with his water pistol;

and, greatly incensed by all the agony of wasted pin curls,
I tackled him, and sat on him, and shot him back—
and then ran home in tears.

Bret fashioned cardboard boxes into castles
inhabited by enviably artistic knights.
He and his friends staged battles—
dumping their knights into a box and stabbing
at them blindly with the sharp end of a compass.
Bret drew a knight for me and played with me
when my folks came to visit his, and kindly
let me forego battles. From boxes, he also created
cowboy towns with banks, saloons, and match-stick jails
inhabited by admirable paper cowboys.
Playing in Wallers' barn loft, the older boys set fires
within their towns, and put them out—
but when young Tommy Waller mimicked them,
he didn't quite—later that afternoon,
the barn burned down.
I saw the smoke and flames from Joan's
and thought my house was burning.

XIII. *The Club*

In her back yard, Joan had a toolshed turned playhouse.
There we girls created a new club each week—
just long enough to elect officers. Our club
was for girls only—except for Tommy Waller—
who was my sidekick, my surrogate little brother.
Once we put on a show in Alice Ann Dechario's attic
(admission: one straight pin, a nod to *Little Women*)
where we performed *The Giggling Girls Gossip Society*,
an inane tea-party interrupted by an imaginary mouse.
We actors were all thrilled when Mr. Lisenbee attended.

XIV. *The Music Teacher*

Mr. Lisenbee conducted our grade school music classes.
He sometimes threatened disobedient students
with a turn across his checkered apron, but the threat
always sufficed—the apron never surfaced.
To choose the songs we sang in class was a big deal—
though David Hunsucker *always* chose
"Grandfather's Clock" or "Atchison, Topeka."
One spring, we did an operetta,
and who-would-be-whose-dancing-partner
was a topic of considerable concern . . .

XV. *Movies*

By fourth grade, kids went, each Friday night,
to the Cozy Theater's double feature.
For fourteen cents, we got
a Batman and Robin serial,
a Disney cartoon,
previews,
a newsreel,
advertisements,
a cowboy (yeah!)
and, finally, a drama to whet romantic fantasies.

Who-had-come-to-sit-with-whom
and whether-they-held-hands
was common knowledge long before
the evening ended and the lights came on.

XVI. *Marlin*

In fourth grade, I had a crush on Marlin Viets.
On spelling tests, we'd race to see who wrote
the word down first, and then look up and smile.

But Mrs. Lloyd said, "Marlin and Mary Kay
must have some kind of secret—
perhaps they'll share it better in the hall."
Bright red at this humiliation! this injustice!
I had to traipse out to the hall with Marlin.

XVII. *Teddy*

Red-haired, freckled, pudgy Teddy Meyer
was my arch rival for head of class.
He and his dad went hunting one winter weekend
and, driving across a railroad intersection,
were hit by a train and killed.
Our class attended their Catholic funeral *en masse*.
Though Teddy and I might well
have been good friends in later years,
we had not been so in fifth grade;
and that compounded the difficulties of this,
my first funeral. The rifle cracks saluting
Teddy's father came like a physical assault
after the unnerving trumpet "Taps."
It was too much—and I withdrew emotionally
from the monstrous sobs of Teddy's
pregnant mother as the two caskets
sank into their graves. That death could come
so suddenly–so tragically–so finally–
to someone *my own age* was terrifying.

XVIII: *Pal*

For years, I'd yearned for two particular things:
a little brother and a pony. When I found Daddy
building a pony stall inside the barn,
I felt that anything I wanted *enough*
just might come true! The day my long-desired,
miraculous pony arrived at last,

Daddy saddled him and helped me mount.
Despite his name, the plump, black Pal
ran off with me immediately. With yells
and threats, Daddy chased after us, while I—
bouncing, jouncing, out of control—
clung to the saddle horn. When Pal stopped short,
I catapulted forward, landed kerplunk!
and couldn't catch my breath.
Mother hired an older boy to ride the pony often,
hoping that exercise would gentle him;
but, when Pal kicked at Daddy,
his days with us were numbered.

XIX: *The Snow-woman*

A letter came from the Adoption Agency:
a social worker, a Mrs. Willamina,
would call on January tenth to talk
about adoption with our family.
I built, in joy and great anticipation,
a wonderful snow-woman with hat, apron,
and carrot nose—a Mrs. Willamina.
The snow delayed the social worker's visit;
but, one noon a few weeks later, she arrived.
Conscious of constructing an impressive,
wholesome scene, I asked for Daddy's help with math.
(Just see! he is so wonderful a father!)
In truth, he was quite good at math and often
helped me see a problem clearly—
and I did need a *little* help that day.

But after my troubled brother came and went,
after Mother's cancer came and came again,
and after Auntie called that Judy was gravely ill . . .

that Judy died, I learned the un-American truth
that wanting didn't necessarily mean getting—
and was a child no longer.

Kay (right) and her cousin Judy

Judy's Death

Gone white, her face contorted
into agonized denial, Mother
set down the phone, missing the cradle.
Dead! Her sister's only child!

My cousin Judy dead—
the red-headed organ prodigy I'd idolized.
I thought about the month I'd stayed with her
in Lawrence when Daddy was in the army—
she'd been like a big sister. I thought
how we had laughed, gasping for breath,
when Uncle Charlie plopped upon the bed where
we were bouncing—and the whole bed collapsed.
Each season, I had loved to wear her outgrown
clothes—stylish, store-bought, expensive—
doubly dear because they had belonged to Judy.
One Christmas she'd sent me a Girl Scout calendar,
and each month's new, enticing picture made
my deprivation keener, my wishes more devout
Girard could have a Girl Scout troop also.
I thought about that week last summer when
we visited our grandparents in Wichita:
we'd stayed up much too late each night
and fabricated tales of fancied boyfriends—
hers always more spectacular than mine.

My aunt sent me a last remembrance of Judy:
her hillbilly band of small glass figurines.
But I—initiate unwilling
into the mysteries of death and grief—
hid them away deep
in my dresser drawer.

The Seamstress

Sewing was my mother's refuge
when Daddy stayed out drinking highballs
with Grandpa and his bakery buddies.
Sewing remained a comfort while she
recuperated from her bouts with cancer,
but she had loved to sew since she was small.

While she rolled my hair in pin curls,
Mother stopped my fidgeting with tales
of sewing through the night to finish formals
for college dances. She told of sewing clothes
for Mary Esther (the German bisque who made brief,
supervised appearances from her safe storage
in our linen closet). That doll was named
for Mother's younger sister who,
with two younger brothers, had died
of ptomaine poisoning within one tragic week.
Mother herself had nearly died,
and spent a year recuperating—perhaps
that was the time she learned to sew
and to find solace in her seams.

I loved the dolls which magically appeared
each Christmas morn with wondrous wardrobes
sewed by Mrs. Santa, but I never sewed for them.
Laboriously, I hemmed a tea towel
as a 4-H project once, but Mother was
too ready to make anything I wanted,
too ready to insist—on those few projects I did try—
that I rip out mistakes and sew things right.
After I grew too old to want new dolls, Mother
continued dressing them to sell or give away.

Once she sent Mrs. Eisenhower a doll—in part
because, as a staunch Kansas Republican,
my mother adored Mamie. But when
Truman Capote wrote how his ancient cousin sent
a homemade Christmas fruitcake to
President Roosevelt as an effort to counter
isolation, to connect with wider, more
"eventful worlds,"* I thought, how true!
That's how it really was.

Each autumn, Mother made me five school dresses—
and choosing their material at Sauers' Department Store
was serious business—as well as an exhilarating
harbinger of school's return. The year my best friend
Joan and I shared a mixed third-and-fourth-grade class,
Joan's daddy died. Her mom went out to work,
so Mother made Joan dresses too.

Each spring, Mother sewed several layettes,
which our church sent to an orphanage in Africa;
and she made aprons and potholders to sell
at church bazaars. She sewed most of the clothes
she wore; and, when I grew to be her size, she
sometimes let me wear them, too—though once
my honest compliments provoked a sharp,
"You can't have *that* one, Mary Kay!"

When I got engaged, I asked Mother
to make my wedding dress. She copied
an elaborate gown from a newspaper
advertisement in *The Kansas City Star*.

---

*Truman Capote, "A Christmas Memory" in *Selected Writings*
(NY: Random, 1963) 154.

My wedding portrait graces still our
back-stairs picture wall—although sometimes
I wonder how many migraines that gown cost.
Years after Mother made that dress—
when every wedding cake she decorated
for Zettl's Bakery sent her to bed for days—
she mentioned how reluctantly she'd undertaken
sewing it, how difficult that dress had been to make.
"Why didn't you say no?" I asked;
"You didn't have to make it!"
She shrugged. "That's not what you say when
your daughter asks you to make her wedding dress."
Believe me, I made sure my daughters
knew this story—knew better than to ask!

Before she died at fifty-eight, Mother sewed,
as much as she was able, for my five children.
By then I'd learned to sew, and to sew well—
and sometimes even to enjoy it.
Yet always my true passion was
for sowing words, symbols, and meanings.

My daughter, Mary, seems to have my mother's
love for fashioning cloth. When Mary was small,
her bouts of tonsilitis often kept her home
from school. To ease her boredom once,
I had her sew a blue and white stuffed dog
and praised the job she did—and Mary's been sewing
ever since. In high school, she, too, stayed up
half the night stitching a formal for the next day's dance.
She sewed her way through a divorce and
job uncertainties; now she, too, makes dresses
for her daughter, and for her daughter's dolls.
I like to watch her tackle the impossible,

work through her problems by creating
beauty in material things. Her passion for
sewing seems to connect the generations.
It is no little gift: this stitching together
past, present, and future—
this modeling immortality.

Poet's mother Billie Zettl circa 1949

Beyond Control

I blundered on my mother diapering Huey
with large, flour-sack, tea towels—his gangly,
seven-year-old's body stretched across the bed.
I blundered out again, indignant, sad, and
feeling vaguely soiled. I remembered getting him
a year ago—all eyes and freckles!
He had no extra clothes, not even underwear.
Daddy and Mother took him shopping—
right there in Topeka—so he could have
a coat to wear as we drove to Girard.
Those first hours in the car, I kept
my arm around this little brother
I had wanted badly.

Later I learned things I'd not noted
that day Huey first came to us from
a long string of foster parents:
his back was scarred, as if someone
had beaten him. He didn't even know
if he liked milk. He lied habitually
and changed the subject whenever
Mother tried to talk with him.
Constantly, he wet the bed and woke,
crying with nightmares. Night after night,
Mother got up to change his sheets and
comfort him. I didn't understand,
until I'd had children myself,
how bone tired, sleep deprived, exhausted,
literally at wit's end a parent gets
from a child's nighttime needs—

and that memorable diaper scene came shortly
after Mother's first cancer operation.

Now I remember Mother fingering the lump
that rose on her breastbone a few months
after we got Huey. And I,
in such a terror she would die,
spent all her operation day in bed myself
with menstrual cramps. At twelve, I was
too young for an official visit; but someone
let me into the hospital in Wichita,
into the room where she lay reeking of anesthetic—
I dashed into the hall and vomited
into a pile of dirty sheets.

My Yard

In our pre-television days, the story plots for kids'
imaginary games came from the books we read
or movies that we watched. My yard became my stage,
my school, my artist's studio, my portal to the heavens.
Donning my cowboy hat, I strapped on my leather holster,
fired my cap pistol or exploded lady-fingers
(if it were near enough the Fourth); robbed, brazenly,
the bank beneath the front-yard maple; and galloped off
with the imaginary loot on my imaginary horse.
My hideout was the old stone steps
and carriage stoop beneath the huge catalpa trees
which lined North Osage Street. There, since I usually
played this game alone, I turned into Gene Autry
or Hopalong and galloped off again in virtuous pursuit.
Sometimes my plots involved a trial that ended in
erroneous conviction, and I explored the gestures,
facial expressions, and emotions of injured innocence.

That front-yard maple—which transformed into
breathtaking royalty each Fall, garbed in a shining
splendor of golds and reds—shaded, with its green canopy,
my summer sand box. There, after rains, I tunneled deep
in the wet sand, built roads and bridges,
sculpted long walls that became forts or buildings,
held wars, and buried small toy soldiers.
Beneath that maple tree, I crafted dolls
from hollyhocks that grew beside our barn.
Inverted, the bright blooms made flowing skirts;
and the spent, shriveled flowers that fell beneath
the hollyhocks' tall stalks made heads and hair for girls
or—partially divided, twisted just so—made pants

for boys, whose heads were the green buds.
The dolls got small twig arms and, sometimes,
an iris-petal cape that looked like purple velvet
and smelled delightfully like grapes.
That maple tree held my rope swing, which I so
loved that Daddy had Samp Roper weld a metal
swing-set for me with bars and a trapeze.
There I hung from my knees and skinned the cat,
bellowed loud snatches of Armed Service songs,
and played I was a paratrooper.
Jumping off bars, I cried, "Bail out!"
climbed up the bars again and cried, "Bail in!"

The grey stone steps and stoop beneath the great catalpas
led to a concrete walk that once connected to a huge,
ramshackle house my parents had replaced with
our white clapboard ranch. Now that sidewalk-to-nowhere
was a place to ride a tricycle or chalk a hopscotch court.
Our address still was 603 North Osage, but our new house
faced south onto Catalpa. In those days (the 1940's and 50's),
the 600 block of North Osage ended at Childers' pond—
the northern edge of town. Our white ranch house
on that block's southeast corner had a large yard with
ample space for kick-base, catch, croquet, or badminton.
Sometimes I simply sat in my yard to read—though
I remember, in early teens, attempting *Les Misérables*
with excellent intentions. Distracted by boy watching,
I reread the bit about the priest and his stolen candlesticks
two or three times before I gave up on that book.

In Daddy's largest garden, we planted vegetables galore;
we had, besides, two patches for asparagus and strawberries.
Picking strawberries was not my favorite chore—
bending over in hot summer sun to rummage

through itchy leaves for red, ripe berries!
But those berries tasted sweeter than any I ever bought.

West of our gardens was our chicken pen, our source
of eggs and meat which, fried in recycled bacon grease,
seemed heavenly—though such fried foods may well
have helped my Grandpa Zettl heaven-wise
a little earlier than normal. Our chicken pen
was even home once to a pig and to a turkey.
Next to the chicken pen, we kept a rabbit hutch,
and we all liked fried rabbit—though, if I balked
at eating pets, my parents might *sometimes* suggest
that this particular meal was a wild rabbit Daddy shot.

In the humongous barn left from the ramshackle house,
Daddy raised pigeons and let me keep (for a short while)
a pony and grow a calf. Quite close behind our house
was a dog pen for Mr. Tax, my daddy's sacred pointer.
My springer spaniel and my cats roamed free—
as was the custom then—poor Penny plagued
by matted cockleburs she picked up in the fields.

I recall Daddy's pouring concrete for a curved front walk.
(I watched him in the fire-fly dusk too long
and wet my pants
and hid them in my dolly buggy
and lied when asked about them later—
and got my mouth washed out with soap.)
But Daddy was on a concrete-pouring roll.
With, perhaps, *some* lack of architectural finesse,
he built, next to the dog pen, a mortar-and-fieldstone fence
between our yard and our north vacant lot;
a mortar-and-fieldstone fishpond, which seldom
was clear of leaves and rarely housed live fish;

and a mortar-and-fieldstone fireplace,
which we used mainly for toasting marshmallows.

I loved, without knowing I loved, the flowers in our yard.
Both red and white spirea bushes edged the house—
a nuisance when we washed our outside windows.
Pink peonies lined the northern flagstone walk,
which led from the side door of our small garage,
to Daddy's mortar-and-fieldstone incinerator
where we burned our trash. The bright blue flowers
Mother called "Wandering Jew" thrived there,
but when we weeded, they were the first to go.
(Their blue is still my favorite color—and sometimes
I think of Wandering Jew and wonder
how it is weeds get defined as weeds . . .)
Nasturtiums and petunias lined the western walk
from that same garage side door out to the chicken pen
and barn. Our driveway came north from Catalpa
toward the southwestern corner of our attached garage
and then curved round before our western walk and barn
to join the alley. That U-shaped drive cut out
an island of clover, dandelions, and thick grass
where Mother's clothesline stood. Pink sweet peas
vined the fence along that island's alley side,
and purple iris lined its driveway curve.
Between the clothesline and the sweet peas was
a long bed of glads—memorable for a game
Mother devised while we were weeding:
We became Stanley's expedition
searching through Africa for Dr. Livingston.
The weeds we pulled were tropical indeed—
in size, in quantity, and in fatigue.

Beside our small front porch, red roses
climbed their trellises, perfuming many a night

when I sat on porch steps, gazing at stars
and constellations—agog at both my insignificance
and my expansive range of possibilities as part
of God's vast, gorgeous universe. Always,
I came inside possessed by a great peace.

When I was twelve, Daddy taught me to use
our power mower. I tried to mow before the morning
got too hot. Our yard was large, and it seemed
monstrous on mowing days. To pass the time,
I sang all of the songs I knew: the ones
from music class at school, church hymns,
the silly songs from camp. Fortunately,
I didn't have to mow our vacant lot for long.

Daddy sold it to Gene Vietti, who built between us
and the Wallers. Before that sale, there was a path
across our vacant lot where, daily, Mother walked
to drink a Coke with her good friend, Juanita;
where Daddy and Mother often went to share
an after-dinner drink or play Parcheesi (nickel a man)
with their dear friends, the Wallers.

The night before I married John and left my home
on North Osage for good, our wedding party sat
on my front porch among fragrant red roses.
As Lucky Heath, John's groomsman, played ukulele,
we sang folk songs, watched stars, and wished
that evening's happiness could last
forever after . . .

Trees

Planted in anticipation that Girard would spread,
two rows of catalpas towered yet
above flat Kansas fields of frost-brown weeds.
There, skirting waist-high cockleburs,
I walked through early adolescence till
winter sunsets transformed that stately
avenue into black supplicants who
raised bare Kilmer arms in a vermillion sky.
Then I went home again absolved—
all angst and anger shrunk smaller
than I, beneath the trees.
Half-way along this avenue, one tree,
its curving branch a natural pew,
invited me to sit,
to run my hands down its rough bark,
to feel nature connecting me with God.

When my brother (adopted after years of want,
my own beloved brother) set fire
a neighbor's porch, I took him walking,
showed him my tree cathedral
and special seat, naively pleaded,
"Come here when you are tempted
to do bad things, and it might help . . ."
But he hid naked in a neighbor's closet
and jumped out at their daughter.

The mental hospital
had bleak white walls
and bare wood floors,
and trees that one might view
through dirty windows—
but not touch.

The Science Teacher

Doc Saccane, shorter even than
my five foot two, was one tall teacher.
He taught us biology and chemistry
in those pre-Sputnik days when science classes
weren't yet dissected by the government.
His glasses magnified the sparkle in his eyes,
and his exuberance was infectious.
Early each semester, he performed
his signature gymnastic feat:
elevating his lithe body at odd angles
from his chair and desk, he demonstrated
his superior skill and discipline.
He introduced us to exquisite worlds:
to species, phyla, systems of ecology and physiology;
to compounds, molecules, and chemical reactions.
These new perspectives danced about my consciousness
like country squares responding to their caller's
intricate commands, like hot-damn jitterbugs
throwing their all into each passionate gyre.
He let Charles Darwin's evolutionary theory
expand, inform my faith, which yearned to love
God with my mind as well as heart and soul.
One of the precepts he chalked daily on our board
I have recalled for years with gratitude
to Doc Saccane, who, by teaching us
to question conclusions critically, taught us
to value modesty and tolerance in others
and in ourselves: *The Truth itself*
never changes—what we believe is true
changes from day to day.

Zettl's Bakery

For me, the family bakery was a great ambivalence.
It furnished magnificently decorated birthday cakes
and—just for the asking—cookies, donuts, candy,
or ice cream. It gave our family sustenance, financial
expectations (including my college education),
and a level of prestige in our small town. It was
the proof of Grandpa's accomplished rise from
immigrant to entrepreneur, of his hard work—
and I adored my Grandpa Zettl!

But my discomforts with the bakery multiplied
as I grew older: In junior high, one of the more
obnoxious boys teased me about the rats that ran
around our shop at night; and then there was
the bakery's toilet—supposedly for workers only—
which often was embarrassingly dirty. There was
the day I noticed one of my black classmates standing
at our counter to collect her lunch and leave.
When I asked why, Mother explained white
customers weren't willing to sit and eat with blacks . . .
Overhearing bits of a conversation once,
I asked *what* were the problems at the Pittsburg shop?
Mother said a union was trying to organize its workers,
and Grandpa and Grandma felt betrayed—their workers
were their family—they didn't want a union making trouble.
There were the German relatives whom Grandpa
brought to America to work—a tit for tat
that sometimes caused hard feelings.

Though Zettl's Bakery made ice cream
and had booths, tables, and a counter where
we sold ice cream concoctions, our customers

came chiefly from the courthouse coffee-and-pastry
crowd mid-mornings, the business hamburger-and-salad
crowd at noon. Late afternoons were slow,
and high school kids stopped at a malt shop two doors down—
until its owner made an impudent, imprudent bet against
the hometown Girard Trojans and all the kids boycotted him.
Mother suggested then I should encourage my friends
to come, instead, to Zettl's Bakery—but I was mortified
at the mere thought and never said a word.

Still, I was thrilled when Daddy asked me—
a sophomore in high school yearning to earn money—
to work in the ice-cream room after his helper quit.
I had to stuff and lock two dozen sticks apiece
into a series of lids and set each lid atop a bar mold
filled by an older worker with vanilla-ice-cream mix.
With a hooked pole, that worker moved the molds
along a channel of cold brine until I could remove
a lid of frozen ice-cream bars. Holding that lid,
I dipped its bars into a waiting pan of liquid chocolate,
inverted it, and lowered it into a monstrous freezer chest
to let the chocolate harden. That freezer was so deep
I had to belly up onto its edge and—
feet flopping in air—lean
down,
down,
down
to reach the bottom.
After I stuck sticks into another lid and set sailing
another mold along its briny path,
I repeated my gymnastic freezer feat,
lifted out that first (now-finished) lid,
and released its bars onto a table.
While a jury-rigged hair drier blew open
sacks, I sacked and boxed the bars,

and put them in the freezer one last time.
This process I repeated hour after hour,
five days a week, all summer.
Daily, I walked home—tired, hot, glad to escape
at last the ice-cream room's frequent ammonia
smell, splattered from head to toe with mix
and melted chocolate, uncomfortably sticky—
not quite so thrilled to be employed
by Zettl's Bakery as I had been at first.
But once I knew the drill, my family
expected me to keep on working . . .

As health and married happiness slipped
through her fragile fingers, Mother occasionally
confided her concerns: that Grandpa had developed
other confidants while Daddy was in the service . . .
that Daddy, though heir-apparent to the shop,
was given no authority.   She fantasized if only Daddy
had a job he truly loved, he'd cut his daily drinking,
he'd cut his constant, escapist hours of television.
"Your life should be about the things you love,"
she preached. Then, suddenly, my Grandpa Zettl
died the March that I was seventeen. That summer
I became Grandma's traveling companion—
a bittersweet escape from making ice-cream bars.
Daddy and Grandma jointly inherited The Bakery—
and all the financial problems for small town bakeries
inherent in the times. For two more summers,
I paid my dues—and wished that I were anywhere but
waiting tables at Zettl's Bakery.

Yesterday, John and I went with our granddaughter
to see the circus. As the day's rain ran underneath
the tent to gully and puddle the dirt floor of their
entrance ring, a family of trapeze performers

tried to keep their hands and slippers dry.
Gingerly, they climbed up, up, up, up,
up toward the canvas ceiling.
The smallest girl (who looked about thirteen)
flipped through the air to a heart-stopping
catch by her muscular grandfather. When she
returned to her trapeze and to the safety of her perch,
she looked *exceedingly* relieved. I shook
my head, nudged John, and murmured,
"I guess I should be grateful
my family's expectations
related to a bakery."

Joe & Marie Zettl in Zettl's Bakery circa 1949

The Baker

Stout grandfather, I have the stein
you earned as an apprentice:
outside, white-aproned *Deutscher* baking bread;
inside—lifting the pewter lid and tilting
towards the light—a shadowy Madonna.
Boldly, your beer stein boasts,
Eher soll die Welt verderben
Als vor Durst ein Bäcker sterben
(Better the world should go to hell first,
than to let a baker be dying of thirst).

You sailed the Atlantic—how goes the story?
fifteen times? Then you jumped ship;
hired to a Pittsburgh Pennsylvania baker;
and there made friends with Bill,
who brought you home to mother—
a nice German boy to marry with his sister.

Then you (Joseph and Marie) sojourned
to Kansas City, where you lived in one room,
sparse furnished with a hot plate, mattress, and
a baby boy—Karl Adolph (both honorable names
in nineteen hundred eleven). Three nights a week,
you scraped together carfare to a part-time job:
baking the daily bread for daily workers—
baking the staff-of-life, mankind's-eternal-food.

You saved, dreamed the infectious dream,
and—helped by a kindly mentor—
bought a small bakery in Girard.
From baskets carried on your back,
you peddled bread on the town square.

From Kansas wheat, from good
white flour and brewer's yeast,
you baked the great white loaves.
(Flour salesman, come, stay with us—stay;
drink with us—drink a highball or two. . .
or three . . . or more . . .)

A child entranced, I watched
the shiny, rubbery dough, rising
in bathtub-like bins, smelling of pungent life.
I watched huge chunks of dough
slapped onto floured tables,
cut, kneaded, and shaped by German nephews,
imported nephews . . . I feel the heat
oppressing me so much I hold my breath and run—
escape the ovens and the racks;
the undershirted, sweating men pulling,
with greyed, singed cloths, pan after pan
of bread from huge, hot ovens—
run toward the slippity-slip machine
that seals the golden bread in cellophane.
Family prerogative, I swipe a crippled loaf and,
pulling out fragrant chunks of soft, white innards,
eat all I can hold of Zettl's bread.

During the 1940's, your bakery grew to three,
each with its marble-crested soda fountain,
where you sold Zettl's Sweetheart ice cream.
You had a fleet of trucks and rode the routes,
exhorting the grocers to cast your loaves
upon their choicest shelves. When a truck's
engine wore out, you used its body
(to my embarrassment, still blazoning our name)
to house pigs on the smelly farm outside of town
where you made use of stale.

Your bakeries survived the Great Depression
and World Wars, before both Pittsburg
and Fort Scott succumbed to television—
competitors who seized the shimmering hour
with smiling rabbits spieling Bunny Bread,
with country-western singing.

One night, carousing with American Legion friends,
you crawled upon a pool table to nap
and found a longer sleep.
For the surviving shop, Karl and Marie
battled changing tastes and changing economics
until their colon cancers came and
the remaining Zettl's Bakery
disappeared.

Now I am back to care for Grandma Zettl as she dies,
back in the little house you lived in years ago.
I read a newspaper account tonight:
"Researchers believe they have confirmed
connections between white flour and
colon cancer . . ." The irony invites despair!

Against my nihilistic thoughts,
I set you, Grandpa Joe:
your will to work,
your love for me,
your zest for life . . .

The Rescue (to John)

We'd gone with Mother while Daddy fed his cows.
As we came out of church, he collared you:
"Heifer's gone through the ice—I need your help!"
We piled into his Olds and sped out to the forty
acres south of town where Daddy raised
his dozen Angus. Roping the heifer,
he kept her head above the gaping pond
while you grabbed hold his ax and
(in dress shoes, suit, and tie) maneuvered
gingerly across the ice to chop an exit path
for the exhausted cow. "Be careful!
Please be careful!" Mother and I chorused.
Finally, the poor creature, eyes rolling in terror,
struggled out onto the snowy bank.
The heifer stood a moment trembling, her soaked
coat spiking icicles in the relentless wind.
Then, with a plaintive moo, she joined the herd,
and we went home to dinner.

Touching Old Scars

How can I write about Girard,
but not of Huey—yet, what can I say?
Blame families' failures, the state's incompetence,
medical ignorance, financial pressures?
Confess my guilt: abandoning my
schizophrenic brother, allowing
fear to govern faith? Accept
tragic reality that illness
can etch the innocent
with a sad, cynic sense of loss?
Any of these might possibly be true.

And yet . . . and yet . . .
the acid complexity of choice
is all I know for sure.
I think— if I had that same
choice to make again
between my sick brother
and my ailing mother,
between my sick brother
and my children's safety—
I would still choose the same,
still mourn the sour necessity to choose.

Then, as I finger these old wounds, I wonder:
like those stretch marks that map my belly
witness to bearing five new lives,
may these soul scars, perhaps,
be marks of bearing human
compassion, sympathy, and love?

Farlington Lake

"To fall asleep," the doctor said, "picture the place
where you felt most relaxed, most comfortable . . ."

So I sit in a rowboat on the lake, and Daddy
pushes off our dock, easing into his customary seat.
Slowly, gently, I row, keeping an even distance
from the shore. He flicks his rod, and his fly ends
its graceful arc precisely where it should:
beside the fallen trees at Norman's dock.
With knowing jerks, he makes it skitter realistically
across the water. The fish aren't hungry yet—
the sun still perches in the treetops of the western shore;
the whippoorwills have yet to conjure up the night.
The boat smells of past conquests—a lakey, fishy
smell I love because of times like these.
When finally we round the cove to fish against
a western bank, the sun has magically
transposed the sky into a giant finger-painting—
great staircase streaks of brilliant orange and red.
Some whippoorwills begin to call, and then
their raspy, twilight concert starts in earnest.
The frogs join in with deep ker-jug-arum!
ker-jug-arum! A cloud of martins swoops across
the sky, their bodies flittering silhouettes against
the softening pinks of growing dusk.
Slowly, silently, I row: dip, pull, and pause . . .
dip, pull, and pause . . . and Daddy casts his line
without a snag—casts, plays, recasts against
the bank beside the buried, fallen trees . . .
Finally, the fish begin to bite—and the mosquitoes!
A sleek snake passes near the boat, almost

Karl "Dutch" Zettl circa 1950

invisible to my inexperienced eye, and Daddy points
that I might see it too. It's growing dark and chilly . . .
I shiver and feel hungry. I think of Mother frying fish,
of hot potato salad, of the big fireplace with its
crackling fire . . . I slap again at the mosquitoes.
When Daddy's finally caught *his* reasonable amount,
he says, "how about some supper?" Gratefully,
I head for home, pulling beneath the stars
across those dark and shining waters full of life—
toward that small dot of light that marks
our cabin's dock. I pull and pull and pull
for all I'm worth—and it is lovely work.

Then, suddenly, I'm grown again and wondering
*What will console my grandchildren when they
can't sleep? Will memories of clean, quiet,
pregnant lakes be there for them?*

Bret Waller

For Mary Lou.
And for Bret Jr., Mimi, Mark, Eric, Brian
and, of course, Eleazarina Slawson-Waller Cat.

North Osage

Spring came Caesarian that year;
excised at last from Winter's grudging womb
she, dying, metamorphosed into Summer.

Catalpas lined our street;
tall, straight ones,
not those crooked dwarfs
you sometimes see,
but towers, thirty, forty meters high,
bedecked in white;
dumb bridesmaids in a double row
they stood, year after year,
awaiting grooms who never once appeared.

Nursing at nippled ends
of blossoms plucked from overladen boughs,
we sucked a honey'd drop from each
and let them fall.

Worn bluestone sidewalks,
white and brown like late spring snow
and slippery with trodden blooms,
gave off the sweet
and slightly sickening musk
of innocence
and adolescent lust.

Later came beans,
catalpa beans, some two feet long
and thick as a boy's thumb!

No good for swordfights
(though we always tried)
they broke too easily,
or bent and dangled limp;
unsatisfactory épées
for d'Artagnan,
and his crowd.

In autumn, it was said,
they could be smoked.
Just cut off both the ends
and light 'em up.

Non-addictive substance,
it appears;
we knew of no bean smoker ever hooked.

Catalpas were always dropping something;
leaves of tobacco size,
like those in Lucky ads.
You didn't rake those up,
but gathered them by hand
like scattered pages from last Sunday's *Star,*
or prayed for wind
to blow them to a neighbor's yard
or take them even farther down the street.

One winter night
an ice storm shrouded
every standing thing with such a shell
that phone lines snapped,
and power lines,
and school was out!

In daybreak light
ice diamonds flashed.
An arctic sun chalked pallid arc
across cerulean skybowl.
Around the silent town,
like rifle shots,
catalpa branches snapped,
came crashing down,
littering snowpacked streets
with crystal shards
that melted the next day.

Grandfather always carried Tums

I remember him as a large man
in a herringbone suit with wide lapels
and a vest stretched tight over his ample middle
making him look exactly like a bloated capitalist
from one of *The Daily Worker*'s editorial cartoons.
But maybe this is just a manufactured memory
derived from a photograph.

I do remember, though,
that he always carried a roll of Tums
in his pocket, and now and again
would slip me one, with a little smile
and a conspiratorial wink.
So now,
when 2 a.m. heartburn
sends me to the medicine cabinet,
the minty taste of Tums
momentarily resurrects him.

We stand together
in Gremma's little rose garden
next to the sunken concrete basin
that sometimes offered glimpses of goldfish.
He, towering above me,
extracts the roll from his pocket,
peels off a minty disk
and slips it to me
with a wink and a smile.

Tadpole

I knew how to do it.
Carefully, carefully to the kitchen sink,
slowly, slowly tip the jar,
hand cupped at the rim,
fingers slightly spread
just enough to let the water trickle out
but not so wide that the tadpole—
The TADPOLE! TADPOLE!
It was so quick, so slippery,
just a touch,
then through my kindergarten fingers
and instantly down the drain!

Remorse, grief, nausea.
Mea culpa! Mea culpa! Mea maxima culpa!
Mother heard my confession when she came home.
"Never mind," she said, "the drain flows down to a stream,
the stream to a river, and the river to the ocean.
He is free and will grow up to be a fine and happy frog."
The ocean was an abstract concept for a Kansas kid,
but the cold, dark hole into which the tadpole disappeared
was very real.
It didn't look like
an escape hatch to the Atlantic.

No larger than a mustard seed,
a grain of doubt
planted thus in a dark place,
began slow gnostic gnaw at truths received:
Tooth Fairy, Santa, Easter Bunny, God.
A double loss, I feel it still:
the slip, too fast for reflex,
the doubt, too deep for reason.

The Coal Shed

Resurrected in memory,
she wears a cotton dress
dotted with tiny pink and blue animals,
or maybe flowers.
More than likely her mother made it;
probably from a feed sack,
as many did in those days.

They live in a bungalow
next to the yellow-stuccoed church,
where her father preaches on Sundays.
Between house and church
a sparse lawn
baked hard by summer sun,
is dappled with dandelions.
She and I are in kindergarten together.

One afternoon
playing at her house,
she invites me into the coal shed—
cool and dark and low, as I remember it,
(though I recall no coal)
slanting light slipping in through cracks
and eddying around the half-open door.
It's quiet.

Then, pointing,
she says coyly,
"I'll show you mine,
if you show me yours."

At first, I don't understand
the proposed transaction,
but when I do,
not wanting to seem
an ungrateful guest,
I drop my pants.

We both stare
for a moment,
at my stubby pink mushroom.

Then,
deftly shedding underwear,
she raises the pink and blue veil,
warbling, triumphantly,
"Ha ha! I don't have any!"

I ascertain
that this is, indeed, the case,
and feel that somehow
I have been the loser
in whatever game we were playing.

Bike Race

John, who lived farthest north,
would show up promptly at seven.
Usually I was ready
and we biked on to Summit for Joe,
who was never ready.

Lightning! we chorused from the curb,
at the top of our adolescent lungs,
Lightning! Come on Dechario!
Eventually Joe emerged,
sleep bleared and rumpled,
and the race was on.

Finish line at the far end of town:
Emerson Junior High,
grim fortress of learning
less hospitable than the Bastille.

Even so, we stood on the pedals
pumping relentlessly all the way
to the crest of a little hill
that gave the first glimpse
of our destination.

There we stopped, caught
our breath and paid respects
to the ancient wraith RAYMOND,
who, we liked to pretend,
was interred beneath a massive
curbstone bearing his name.

It was always Joe and John
jockeying for the lead, while I,
consumed with envy and frustration,
struggled behind, silently
cursing my mongrel velocipede
cobbled together during the War years
(when even bikes were rationed)
from cannibalized carcasses of
Schwinn, Hawthorn, Silver King,
and god knows what other makes
and models. Like Frankenstein's monster,
a victim of mismatched parts,
my ungainly contrivance crept crabwise
with groaning reluctance.

When I pulled up—last again, and winded—
my buddies, already breathing normally,
had air enough to laugh
and restart our sprint toward whatever
the day ahead might hold.

Friday Evening Serials

In those pre-Spandex days
Superman's tights sagged,
and in black and white
they looked a lot like long johns,
lacking the backflap.

And when he flew, it was so fake!
He would stand there, raise his arms,
shout, "Up, up and awaaay!"
and take a little hop,
whereupon they would immediately
cut to a shot of him horizontal
on some hidden board,
with his arms out in front
and a fan blowing in his face
to make his cape flap.

Despite these evident shortcomings,
we never missed an episode.

Sometimes the lead would be Buster Crabbe,
who played different heroes in different series,
so we never heard his real name spoken
and, consequently, never knew whether or not
to pronounce the "e"
at the end.

Probably we fought about that on the way home.
We fought about everything,
and anything; fought for the fun of fighting;
fought because we were young males
crazed by having sat more or less quietly for at least an hour

in the dank, warm, popcorn-scented womb of the Cozy.
So, born again,
heading home,
making our way up Summit Street
in summer darkness,
for an indifferent audience of elderly watchers
in swings and rockers
on their front porches,
nearly invisible, but for the orange glow
here and there, of the tip
of a Camel or a Lucky,
we staged a running reenactment
of whatever battles we had just witnessed.

Jim, who, on Friday nights a few years later,
quarterbacked our high school team,
usually got to be the hero,
at least in his own mind,
though in reality
there were no assigned roles—
each of us
secretly heroic,
rescuing Lois, or Rachel,
or whichever swooning lovely
needed saving.

Grass stains, sweat,
skinned elbows and ripped shirts
were trophies we brought home—
badges of honor proudly won
in Friday evening combats.

Bruenjes' Hand

Gangly,
too large already
for the grade school desk,
lank Bruenjes sprawled,
arm dangling,
veins in the back of his hand
pulsing in *alto relievo,*
like David's
in the *Accademia.*

My fifth-grade arm,
similarly draped,
raised no such vascular topography,
though I watched hopefully for long minutes.

Now, however,
bulging blue through crepe-thin *dermae,*
elevations emerge rivaling those of the snaking Andes
on that long-ago classroom globe.

Familiar as the back of your hand,
which is to say, not familiar at all;
strange, alien appendage.
My face I would know anywhere,
but my hand?
I doubt I could pick it
out of a lineup.

I might even mistake it today
for Bruenjes' hand.

I saw one fall once

You don't think of them falling,
but they do. At least, this one did.
He was way up in the top of one of those
giant catalpas lining North Osage
when I guess he lost his footing
and just came straight down
smack in the middle of the street.
Fortunately there were no cars coming.
I thought he was dead,
but after lying there a couple of seconds
he got up, shook his head, as if to clear it,
and went scampering back up the tree.

On the way down
he sort of spread-eagled,
the way parachutists do in free fall
to keep from tumbling out of control,
so he landed flat on his belly
with legs and tail stretched straight out.
Looked a lot like roadkill.

I sometimes wonder what he thought about
on the way down. Did his little squirrel life
flash before his eyes? And, if so,
what were the memorable episodes?
Did he think of Mama? Gathering acorns?
Chasing and being chased by siblings?
Hibernating? Tormenting the poor, stupid spaniel
that barked itself hoarse whenever a squirrel appeared?
Or, did he just think, *oh, shit,*
now you've done it?
Probably the latter, though I'm not sure
how you would say that in squirrel.

Last Battle

Then the King got his spear in both his hands
and ran toward Sir Modred, crying and saying,
'Traitor, now is thy death day come!'
                    Le Morte Darthur
                    Sir Thomas Malory

A sopping glob of red crepe paper gore
erupted as vile Modred, disemboweled
by fatal pencil (thrust as Arthur's lance)
and skewered like kebob, yet struck a blow
(administered by careful scissors snip)
that cleft his father's crown and brought him low.

There had been wars before, and skirmishes,
enacted upon other battlefields,
but that was bloodless carnage carried out,
for the most part, on nameless knaves
penciled furtively in study halls
and destined for wastepaper basket graves.

This was not that. This was the final fall
of all that had been fabled Camelot,
of all the noble knights of Table Round
of all the games and fantasies of youth
which until now had occupied our days
but had at last to end, we knew in truth.

Thus upstairs sleeping porch linoleum
became the bloody field of Barham Down
and sluice of water and crepe paper pulp
supplied essential sanguinary look

so that each dubbed and designated knight
might meet his fate exactly by the book.

For Joe had read entire *Le Morte Darthur*
and knew precisely how each one expired,
how Gawain died when smitten on the wound
he had received afore from Lancelot,
how Lucan perished frothing at the mouth
and Bedivere, sore wounded, yet did not.

So, as the summer afternoon wore on
the battlefloor became a flood of red
upon which many famous heroes sprawled
ensanguined and unshriven where they fell
and Joe and I pressed on with heavy hearts
for we had drawn them all and knew them well.

And when at last it ended, Joe produced
a marbled cardboard envelope—a tomb
on which he had inscribed in gothic script
the solemn epitaph *Hic iacet Arthurus,*
meaning, he explained, "Here Arthur lies,"
and also *rex quondam rexque futurus.*

The latter, meaning "once and future king,"
appeared to hold out hope of a return,
but we both knew that once a thing has passed
it never comes again, except perhaps
in waking dreams of old, forgetful men
when all but the most ancient memories lapse.

Miss Jane

The only time I ever saw her laugh
        was once in algebra class
when I accidentally stuck a pencil
        up my nose, abstractedly
trying to brush away an annoyingly persistent
        little housefly.

Not really a laugh so much as an instantaneous,
        reflexive exhalation of breath
through the nose—a sort of silent snort—and the flash
        of preternaturally white dentures
usually concealed by lips kept primly pressed
        evincing self-control.

No one else in the class appeared to notice,
        being tangled in algebraic jungles,
so this inadvertent sight gag seemed to me
        to have become our little secret.
I never mentioned it to her, nor she to me,
        but I liked her better for it.

Championship Season 1953

As a linebacker I was clueless,
knowing only that from time to time
a runner would come barreling at me,
and I was supposed to stop him.
Sometimes I did.

Pudge's encouragement from the sidelines
still rings in my ears: *Waller, you Big Meathead!*

Coach also told me
that sometimes a pass would be thrown
(though when and why remained a mystery)
and on such occasions,
my job was to cover the "flat,"
which, he indicated,
was off to the side.

In the final seconds of the game
we're leading by a touchdown,
and McCormick says *it'll be a pass*.
I go out in the flat with a receiver
who breaks downfield,
so I follow, turning at the goal line
just in time to see a Hail Mary
spiraling right into my hands!
Miraculously, I catch it
and have one foot raised to launch
the splendid runback I have dreamt of
when a tackler creams me.
Again miraculously,
I don't fumble the only interception of my career,
but lie on my back clutching the ball
as teammates celebrate far down the field.

My buddy Ed runs up, fearing I'm injured,
but I'm just lying there laughing.
That's not, I gasp, as Ed helps me up,
how I imagined it.

Next day the **Pittsburg Sun**
reports an interception on the last play of the game
by an unidentified player.

The Unidentified Player

Stitchery

Gabled, shuttered,
dark house in a dark woods,
roughed out in woolen cross stitch,
sullen browns, drab greens and grays,
framed above the mantel in the dark room—
it frightened me.

"Did you know your mother made that?"
asked Gremma, proudly, anxiously,
fearing I had forgotten
since she last asked me
a minute earlier.

II.

"Have you ever heard this?"
asked Grandfather again,
and then, again without waiting for reply,
began again banging out "Chopsticks"
on the black upright
in a dark corner
of the dark room.

III.

Did I tell you that yesterday,
in our house in the dark woods,
as I (now, in turn, a grandfather)
varnished window frames,
all morning long
under my breath
I whistled "Chopsticks"?

Inheritance

In the end they had to tell all the merchants around the square
not to sell him anything, not to sell him electric shavers
because he already had a dozen but couldn't remember
any of them, couldn't remember buying them,
couldn't remember using them, couldn't even remember
what they were for—electric shavers.

There was an upstairs room with a step-down in the middle—
lined by those dark oak bookcases with lift-up glass fronts,
that held all his law books. And beyond the sunken law court,
a bathroom with scented soaps and bottles of liquids
the likes of which I had never smelled before; shaving lotions,
I suppose, though that was long before Aqua Velva.

Grandfather was a Republican and a Mason and a university
graduate with a law degree and for a time a state representative and president
of the Chamber of Commerce and an entrepreneur and an inventor with
many patents and finally a fat old man who couldn't be trusted to spend his
own money in any of the shops around the square.

Not that he had any money left to spend. That was the sad part,
though by then he was well beyond being saddened by it.
Father had to pull the company back from the edge of oblivion.
Mother took over as secretary, typing all those "Perfection Line" letters on
100% bond stationery interleaved with carbon sheets and yellow pulp backups
that would have survived perhaps thirty or forty years, had the shop lasted
that long.

Grandfather passed without knowing it. Gremma, too, after
years of wilting in the wanderness, finally subsided.

Dad was done in by bone cancer before he'd even had a chance
to retire to Cuchara and die trout fishing. Mother,
being tougher than any of them, hung on for decades after
her mind had departed.

I do these exercises late at night in the hope of warding off
whatever god or demon calls down upon my clan
the curse of forgetfulness. It could be worse, I suppose.
He might invoke the curse of remembering.

Sketching at the Blue Moon

Unlike Lautrec, I lacked no length of leg;
the Blue Moon Ballroom wasn't Moulin Rouge,
polka and schottish were all the band could manage
there, while Bud and Pabst of the 3-point-2 variety
stood in for pernod and absinthe in dust dry Kansas.

But it was dark in the balcony overlooking the dance floor,
so you could sketch without attracting a lot of attention,
and after a couple of beers could begin to feel
the kind of exquisite artistic alienation that
surely fueled Henri's besotted genius.

Besides, I couldn't dance. So, in the dark
I sketched and, barely glancing at the page,
let instinct lead and guide the hand so as
to interpose no conscious thought between
impulse and act. I was a seismograph.

Viewed in retrospect, the previous evening's
erratic trackings seemed to record
more accurately the rate of beer consumption
than a sensitive soul's response to external stimuli.
But what the hell, I said I couldn't dance.

Nightswim

One boozy nocturnal skinnydipper—
when the long arm of the law
attached to a fat fist clutching a flashlight
suddenly appeared around the corner
of the bath house—attempted to conceal
himself in the 6-inch deep footwasher.

The rest of us, already in the pool,
submerged and stayed under until
our breath ran out, whereupon,
one by one, we breached
like so many killer whales
or porpoises or maybe manatees
(being Kansans, we couldn't know which)
gulped air, and dived again.

This hide-and-seek in abruptly arctic waters
went on for several eternities
until at last the torch bearer seemed
to disappear and I made a run for it
only to be apprehended, flat on my belly
and naked as a jaybird, between
the pool's edge and the chainlink fence
outside of which lay our garments.

Awright,
                    he yelled, accentuating his annoyance
by peppering my backside with a fistful of gravel,

come on out, I gotcha.
                    I meekly complied,
all beery bravado washed away in the frigid
depths of the city pool in Winston park.

Whachername?
                    Prevented from speaking by
a confluence of Bud, fear and hypothermia,
I retrieved from my recovered billfold
what I thought was my Selective Service card,
except it wasn't, being instead one
passed down to me by an older schoolmate
to facilitate the purchase of beer,
which then in Kansas was available
only to those three years older
than you had to be to bear arms
against your country's enemies.

Awright, Hedrick,
                    he growled,
making me instantly aware
that I had compounded the offense
of trespassing, by surrendering a
document the possession of which
probably warranted twenty-to-life.

Awright, Hedrick,
                    he reiterated,
gitcherassouttahere an donneverletmekechyahereagin.

Once more I complied, alternating waves
of relief and nausea competing for dominance
as I struggled to pull tangled jeans
over prunewrinkled chlorinated gooseflesh.

Yessirofficer,
                    I mumbled, finding my voice at last,
Iwonteverletchacatchmehereagain.
                    And I was as good as my word.

I Saw My Father Old

Was I—what—in college?
Or later?
Yes, probably later,
because I had come home from somewhere
after a long absence.

Night, or early morning—
I can't remember which—
he, shuffling along, to the bathroom maybe,
wearing undershorts, probably,
bent,
hair mussed (much missing)
chest fallen, legs so thin,
skin bunched at elbows
a man I didn't know:
my father,
old.
A picture I do not wish to hold.
The one I want,
the one I call to mind
to block out that surveillance camera ghost:
up from the stream
a string of trout held proudly out
fedora brim flipped back
he beams.

This morning,
warm from bed,
muddled still with sleep,
passing the tall glass
in the dressing room,
I saw my father,
old.

The Ice Pond

It would start with the first hint of Spring
when pond water lagged behind
the sun-warmed air. At times
there were three or even four of us,
but usually Ed and I opened the season.

Once there was still a thin scrim
of ice fringing the pond when the games
got underway. Later in summer
losing your footing didn't hurt
much—just the sting of defeat—

but early on, when the water was
near freezing, it sucked your breath
away, turning you blue in the
moments it took to scramble
back to safety on the raft.

Navy surplus I think it was:
elongated "O" of foot-thick balsa
wrapped in wide, rough tape,
a central latticed wooden deck
having long since sunk,

and waterlogged, with two or more
young warriors at one end
it dipped, so that keeping your footing became
even more of a challenge. The rules
were simple: you fall off, you lose.

Through spring and summer, into fall
we jousted, breaking now and again
to sun, and watch the bluegills bunched
piranha-like around the ring
waiting for god knows what.

A lifetime later the raft has disappeared.
Balsa, like everything else, eventually
sinks. Ed lost his footing first
this time around. Tiger went next,
and one-by-one we follow.

The ice-pond water is cold
this time of year.

Gangsters 1952

Front, left to right: Bret Waller, Jim McCormick
Rear: Jack Mills, Ron Breneman, Leroy Purkey

Biographical Notes: Thomas Lisenbee

Born Thomas Rex Lisenbee to Lola Evelyn Lisenbee and Percy Rex Lisenbee on September 20th, 1938 in Girard Hospital (attending physician Doc Lightfoot) a.k.a. Tommy, Rex, Percy, Lizard and god knows what else behind his back, probably known as just plain lazy and ornery by his teachers, Tom left Girard and Osage Street for good in 1960 to make a place for himself in the world of music.

Blessed with just enough talent and more than his share of luck, he had the great good fortune to make a success of it, starting in the Tulsa Philharmonic, then moving on to Europe, doing stints with the Concertgebouworkest of Amsterdam, the Israel Philharmonic, the Radio-Eireann Symphony Orchestra before returning to the United States in 1966 for a successful career freelancing in New York City, where he resides to this day. He retired from trumpet playing in 2001 and now devotes his artistic energies to writing.

His writings, both poetry and fiction, regularly appear in literary journals. In 2006, one of his short stories was short-listed for the Raymond Carver Short Story Prize. He has published one chapbook of poetry, *Dogwalking* (Wild Pines Press), is working on his first novel and, if the stars align themselves just right, who knows, might even find a publisher. He is a member of the Upper Delaware Writers Collective. Tom would love to hear from readers of this book and may be contacted through his website, *www.thomaslisenbee.com* or more directly at TLise22649@aol.com.

Biographical Notes: Kay Z. Myers

Kay Z. Myers (nee Mary Kay Zettl) began our interview with a tale of her two church friends: "Anne laughed as she described how Betty introduced herself at their Cursillo weekend: 'People sat in a big circle and took turns telling about themselves. When it was Betty's turn, *she claimed she'd been a ballerina on the New York stage!*' I gasped, 'But, Betty, why?' 'Oh,' Betty said, 'the others led such interesting lives!' Well, reading Tom's and Bret's biographies in *Three from Osage Street*, I've finally understood how Betty felt."

Then Kay regaled me with tales of her and her husband's adventures: backpacking 100 miles at Philmont Boy Scout Ranch, finding 6,000 pottery shards on an Earthwatch archeology dig, camping cross-continent with their five youngsters on a three-month "Great Trip!" And that improbable story of their move East—John jumping off the train to get last bags and being left behind, while Kay (zombie-like) held their baby on the train for 16 hours. After Kay's Cursillo introduction, what was I to think? I tell you, writers are prone to fiction—even when they're posing as poets and biographers.

"Just stick to the facts please, Ma'am," I begged; and so she finally did: Kay met John Adams Myers at Kansas University; and, in June of 1958, they were married in Girard. During their next five years in Lawrence, Kansas, Kay got her BS in education, John got his PhD in chemical engineering, and they begot three children. In 1963, they moved to Pennsylvania, where John taught at Villanova University. Shortly, they bought the old Victorian in Wayne where they still live.

As two more children and John's mother joined their family, Kay wrote whenever she found time. At Villanova, she took two independent studies in writing and earned an MA in Teaching of English. In 1984, she published fifty early poems in *Philadelphia Marathon* (Wyndham Hall Press). Later, she taught writing and literature part time at Harcum Jr. College and Cabrini College, earned a PhD in English literature from the University of Delaware, and served three years as volunteer coordinator for a 1997 exhibition—*Art & Religion: The Many Faces of Faith*. When that show ended, she wrote separate poems for each of its hundred artists. Recently, she wrote six fairy tales for grandchildren. She says working with Tom and Bret on *Three from Osage Street* has been a joy.

—by Casey Maiers

Biographical Notes: Bret Waller

Although he has attempted poetry since childhood, Bret Waller's chief literary efforts over several decades have been in the fields of art and art history. As director of art museums at the universities of Kansas, Michigan and Rochester, New York, head of public education at the Metropolitan Museum, associate director of the J. Paul Getty Museum and for eleven years director of the Indianapolis Museum of Art, he has contributed essays to scholarly journals, professional publications and numerous exhibition catalogues.

Among his publications are catalogue essays in *The School for Scandal: Thomas Rowlandson's London*; *Artists of La Revue Blanche*; *Works from the Collection of Herbert and Dorothy Vogel;* and articles in scholarly journals on Georges Rouault, Tom Wesselmann, John Steuart Curry and others. Waller has written and has seen produced a one-act play based on the famous legal dispute between James A. McNeill Whistler and John Ruskin. He proudly states, however, that his *magnum opus* to date is a huge corpus of finely crafted and as yet unpublished administrative memos.

Since his retirement in 2000 from the Indianapolis Museum of Art, of which he now is Director Emeritus, Waller has devoted much of his time to efforts at poetry. Many of his poems, like those of his friends Tom Lisenbee and Kay Myers, are devoted to experiences of childhood and youth in his home town of Girard, Kansas. The results of some of these efforts are to be found in the preceding pages.